The Incredible
Atlantic Herring

THE INCREDIBLE ATLANTIC HERRING

Joseph J. Cook

*Illustrated with photographs, old prints,
and drawings*

DODD, MEAD & COMPANY / NEW YORK

ILLUSTRATIONS COURTESY OF: Consulate General of the Netherlands, 56; Jan Cook, 18, 19, 20 *right*, 26, 43; Paul Earl, National Marine Fisheries Service, 49; Fisheries & Marine Service, Canada, 12, 44 *right*, 45 *left* and *top right*, 50; Irish Sea Fisheries Board, 37; Maine Department of Marine Resources, 20 *left*, 33, 34, 35, 40 *right*, 48, 51; Museum of Fine Arts, Boston, Bequest of George Nixon Black by exchange, 38 *right*; Norwegian Information Service in the United States, 17, 23, 25 *right*, 42, 53, 60, 62; Nova Scotia Communication & Information Service, 41; Harold Wes Pratt, National Marine Fisheries Service, 8; W. F. Rathjen, National Marine Fisheries Service, 45 *bottom*, 46, 47, 58; Swedish Information Service, 1, 2, 15, 38 *left*, 40 *left*, 44 *left*, 55.

Frontispiece: Ring-net fishermen hoisting a dip net brimming with Atlantic herring

1   2   3   4   5   6   7   8   9   10

Library of Congress Cataloging in Publication Data

Cook, Joseph J
The incredible Atlantic herring.

Includes index.
SUMMARY: Discusses the Atlantic herring, the
most plentiful, most hunted, and most valuable
food fish found in the North Atlantic.
1.   Herring—Juvenile literature.   2.   Herring-
fisheries—Juvenile literature.   [1.   Herring.
2.   Fishes]   I.   Title.
QL638.C64C73   597'.55   78–24540
ISBN 0–396–07647–5

To M. Jerome Loizzo

ACKNOWLEDGMENTS

The author wishes to thank: Warren F. Rathjen, Chief, Fisheries Development Services Program, U.S. Department of Commerce, National Marine Fisheries Service, Gloucester, Massachusetts; Paul Earl, Assistant Program Manager, New England Fisheries Development Program, U.S. Department of Commerce, National Marine Fisheries Service, Gloucester, Massachusetts; Harold Wes Pratt, Fishery Biologist, Northeast Fisheries Center, U.S. Department of Commerce, National Marine Fisheries Service, Narragansett, Rhode Island; Maine, Department of Marine Resources; John T. Hughes, Marine Fisheries Biologist, State Lobster Hatchery and Research Station, Vineyard Haven, Massachusetts; R. A. Meaney, Assistant Fisheries Development Manager, Irish Sea Fisheries Board; Mark Maritato, Peter McKibbin, and Joseph Zaleski for their assistance in making this book possible.

Contents

I. Atlantic Herring

Swimming swiftly through the chilled, wave-tossed seas of the North Atlantic ocean are fish scientifically named *Clupea harengus*. The species *Clupea harengus*, commonly called Atlantic herring, is known to gather in huge schools of over a billion individuals covering more than six square miles of sea. Such awesome schools have made the Atlantic herring the most plentiful, most hunted, and most valuable food fish in the North Atlantic.

Clupea harengus, a primitive fish that has lived on earth some 150 million years, is divided into numerous races. Each race lives apart from the others and each spawns in a different season, but all the races are similar to one another in every other way. The many races of *Clupea harengus* spend their entire lives in the seas hugging the shorelines of northern Europe and North America.

In Europe, Atlantic herring range from the Arctic coasts of the Soviet Union and Norway into the Baltic Sea, and along the shores of Scotland, Ireland, and England to the northern coastline of Spain.

Photo taken in three feet of water shows part of a school of seven-to nine-inch herring breaking formation to swim around a dock

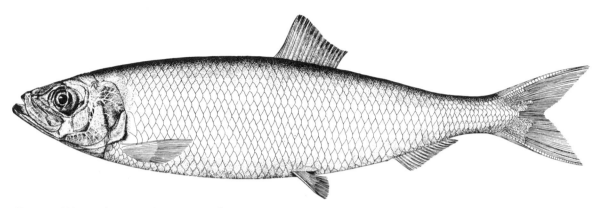

Herring *(Clupea harengus)*. From Goode. Drawing by H. L. Todd

In North America, *Clupea harengus* ranges from Greenland south along the coast of North America from Labrador to Virginia. But the largest numbers are found north of Block Island, a small island situated off but part of Rhode Island, to Newfoundland.

An Atlantic herring has a blue-green back, silvery sides, and a white belly. The fish, measuring in length up to eighteen inches and up to a pound and a half in weight, is built for sustained speed with tapered head and a long, compressed body. The mouth is large, with the lower jaw projecting over the upper jaw. Nostrils, set in the snout, are used for scenting, not breathing. As is true with all fishes, an Atlantic herring breathes by absorbing oxygen from the water pouring into its mouth and out openings called gills. A gill is located on each side of the body at the rear of the head. In the gills are delicate, threadlike tissues called filaments. When water passes over the gills, oxygen in the water is diffused by blood coursing through the filaments. Hemoglobin, a pigment found in the red blood cells, "traps" or "catches" the oxygen. Once trapped, the oxygen is chemically changed to oxyhemoglobin and circulated throughout the body.

The eyes of an Atlantic herring, large and set wide apart on the head, have poor frontal but excellent side vision. Ears, set behind the eyes, are keen and pick up sound vibrations in the water. Both the eyes and ears are used not only for sight and sound but also for balance as the Atlantic herring swims in seas of calm or storm, day and night.

Halfway along the body of an Atlantic herring are the dorsal and ventral fins. The dorsal fin, located on the back, is short and soft, not spiny. On the belly, opposite the dorsal fin, are two soft ventral fins. Behind the ventral fins is a soft anal fin. Two soft pectoral fins, situated on each side of the body near the gill openings, are immovable. Most fishes have movable pectoral fins that help them in steering and stopping. An Atlantic herring, having immovable pectoral fins, is unable to stop quickly, reverse, or hover in the water. However, it is able to veer left or right and move up and down in the water while swimming. The soft caudal fin or tail of an Atlantic herring is deeply forked. Such deeply forked tails on fishes generally indicate great speed, and an Atlantic herring is no exception to this general rule. It is capable of swimming long distances at speeds up to twenty knots.

Atlantic herring in the hold of a fishing ship

Covering the body, except for the head and fins, are large, curved scales that meet at the belly, forming a keel-like structure. The scales protect the skin and flesh from both the infections caused by slashing jaws of predators and the boring action of certain unhealthy parasitic and bacterial life found in the sea. Each scale, smooth rimmed and shaped somewhat like a human fingernail, has the front end loosely tucked into the skin while the rear portion is free. Because the scales are loosely attached to the skin they are easily rubbed off, but new ones do grow to replace any that are dislodged.

The number of scales that an Atlantic herring has at birth is the same number it will have at death. The scales grow in proportion to the fish's growth. Although an Atlantic herring may live twenty years, body and scale growth is greatly reduced when it reaches maturity at approximately three years of age.

2. The Natural History of Atlantic Herring

Mature Atlantic herring are approximately eight to ten inches long. The reproductive organs, situated near the kidneys, are fully developed. Testes in the males are capable of producing sperm, and ovaries in the females are able to produce eggs.

The majority of fishes, including Atlantic herring, give birth to their young by spawning. Spawning occurs when males and females of a species have fertile or life-giving sex cells. The sex cells are shed or deposited into the water. Fertilization, the fusion or union of sperm and egg, then immediately takes place in the water.

Immense schools of Atlantic herring form when the eggs of the females, swollen and ripe, are ready to be shed. Scientists have estimated that a spawning school may contain 500 million males and females in one square mile of sea. Gathering in the millions, the herrings cover vast surfaces of the open sea as the schools move shoreward to spawn. All members of a school are approximately the same age and size. Slightly larger or smaller fish form their own schools, as the swimming speed of Atlantic herring varies depending upon the size of the fish.

Herring *(Clupea harengus)*, from Goode, drawing by H. L.
Todd, assembled by Salem Tamer to show swimming formation

Schools of Atlantic herring seem to move in precise formation. Each fish's head is halfway between the head and tail of the fish to its right and left. The schools are so tightly packed together that no fish can turn left or right without hitting another. Fishes such as bluefish, mackerel, bluefin tuna, yellowfin tuna, and bonito slash into the enormous schools to feed on the herring. Marine mammals such as porpoises, seals, and finback whales also come to satisfy their hunger. Pieces of herring flesh not swallowed by the feeding fishes and mammals bob to the surface where diving birds scoop

14

them up. Relentlessly, the ever-moving schools swim shoreward. As the herring near the spawning grounds, man, the most powerful predator on land or sea, makes his appearance in boats to hunt the fattened, mature food fish.

When the survivors in the schools reach the spawning grounds, usually in waters less than 300 feet deep, the females release clusters of hard, smooth, sticky eggs while swimming on their sides over and around rocks, stones, and other clean debris. The females usually shed no more than 20,000 to 40,000 eggs each year. This is a smaller amount of eggs than most female sea fishes discharge. However, the vast numbers of

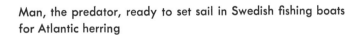
Man, the predator, ready to set sail in Swedish fishing boats for Atlantic herring

female Atlantic herring make up for the small number of eggs shed. Unlike most marine fishes, whose eggs are small and buoyant, Atlantic herring eggs are heavy and quickly sink to the bottom. Sinking and clinging to debris on the floor of the sea saves many of the eggs from attack and devastation by surface-feeding predators. Although safer on the bottom of the sea than on the top, the eggs are still open to attack by such bottom-feeding fishes as cod, hake, and haddock.

Atlantic herring males, closely following the females, discharge clouds of sperm into the water. Slowly the sperm settles on the eggs. Both males and females, after casting their sex cells into the sea, swim on. There is no parental care for any young that may be born.

Following the successful penetration of an egg by sperm, the life cycle of an Atlantic herring begins. A fertilized egg incubates for ten to forty days. The colder the temperature of the water the longer it takes for an egg to develop. Therefore, the warmer the water the sooner the egg will hatch.

The birth of an Atlantic herring occurs when the tiny, transparent creature hatches from a fertilized egg. Looking entirely unlike its parents, the frail, huge-eyed offspring is called a larva. Somewhat resembling an insect, the larva has the yolk sac of the egg from which it hatched still attached to it. The yolk sac is the larva's first food. After absorbing it, the larva, measuring less than half an inch, rises to the surface of the sea by wiggling its tail. At the sea's surface the hatchling joins a multitude of tiny plant and animal life collectively called plankton.

The word plankton comes from the Greek language and means wandering. Plankton, having little or no locomotion, wanders or floats passively on or near the surface of the sea. This "soup" of tiny plant and animal life is the staff of life for all creatures that live in the sea. Fishes and sea mammals that do not feed directly on the minute organisms feed on sea life whose diet is either partially or exclusively plankton. Without plankton the sea would soon be a watery desert.

The life cycle of plankton begins in late winter and early spring. Melting snows and pelting rains gush, flow, or trickle into rivers, streams, and brooks, washing mineral particles from the earth seaward. Pouring into estuaries that flow into the sea, the mineral specks slowly reach the depths of the ocean. Frigid North Atlantic surface water, blanketed by dark, moody skies and buffeted by winter storms and early spring tides,

Runoff water from snow carries mineral specks, basis for the chain of life in the sea

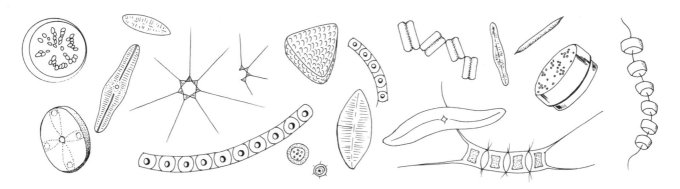

Some varieties of the tiny plants called phytoplankton are shown here highly magnified

becomes heavy and sinks, just as cold air settles on the floor of a room. As the chilled surface water sinks, warmer water lying in the depths rises, as hot air rises in a room. The rising water brings with it not only the washed-down land minerals but the mineral remains of dead sea life that rested on the bottom during the long, somber winter season.

With the rise in water temperature, surfaces of the sea soon blossom into vast, undulating meadows of tiny plants called phytoplankton. Phytoplankton, although spending its entire life floating at or near the surface of the sea, lives much as grass does on land. Like grass, phytoplankton depends on the sun's energy for its ability to change minerals into food and oxygen. This ability or process, scientifically named photosynthesis, is basically the same for both grass and phytoplankton. It is the

18

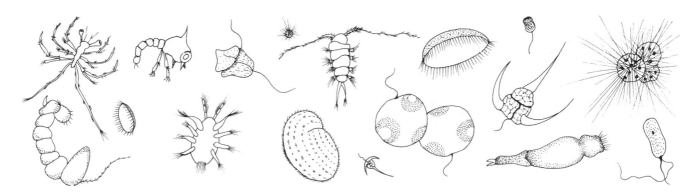

These examples of zooplankton—one-celled animals—are greatly enlarged

phytoplankton which converts the washed-down mineral particles from the earth and the mineral remains of dead sea life floating in the sea into food and oxygen.

With summer's approach, zooplankton—one-celled animals—and the larvae or young of mollusks and crustaceans such as oysters and lobsters which are born at the bottom of the sea in spring rise to the ocean's surface to feed on the phytoplankton. During the day these minute plants and animals settle beneath the surface to escape the direct rays of the sun. At night the organisms float to the surface to get light cast from the moon and stars.

Joining the floating fields of plankton, the hatched Atlantic herring larvae are prey to many predators. Gulls and other sea birds can easily pluck floating larvae from the sea's surface. Also, surface-feeding fishes and sea mammals, consuming vast amounts

Lookout spotting a school of Atlantic herring

Below: Herring cycle

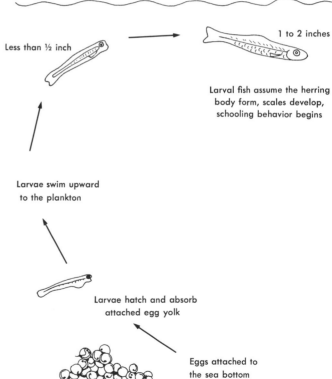

Less than ½ inch

1 to 2 inches

Larval fish assume the herring body form, scales develop, schooling behavior begins

Larvae swim upward to the plankton

Larvae hatch and absorb attached egg yolk

Eggs attached to the sea bottom

of plankton, swallow large quantities of larvae.

Growth of the surviving herring larvae is dependent upon many factors. One extremely important determinant is the salinity or saltiness of the water, which is often influenced by the amounts of fresh water flowing from the land into the sea. Large amounts of fresh water decrease the salinity level of sea water. Herring larvae prefer seas of high salinity and reach adult form sooner in such waters than in seas of low salinity.

Drifting on the rolling, windswept seas of autumn off the New England coastline, eggs spawned in August, hatched in November, may in April average one or two inches in length. At this stage larvae begin to assume the typical Atlantic herring shape. Scales start to form and the instinctual schooling behavior of the species asserts itself. Schools of tiny Atlantic herring now feed on the plankton of which they were once part.

By feeding on plankton, an Atlantic herring is one of a number of sea fishes to change tiny plant and animal life into solid flesh. But, by feeding on plankton, which is defenseless, an Atlantic herring is not an active hunter. It does not have to attack and battle other sea creatures in order to eat and survive. Rather, it is the herring that is hunted by scores of predators.

From a bird's eye view above the blue-green water or a fish or sea mammal's eye view looking up from below, the Atlantic herring's iridescent blue-green back or its silvery-white belly provide protective coloration, depending on which way the eye is looking. By grouping in large schools, an Atlantic herring is performing an instinctive protection act in accordance with nature's design. Although many individuals in the school will be killed, enough should survive to ensure the survival of the species.

An Atlantic herring, with jaws set wide apart, cruises the seas, filtering oxygen and plankton from the water entering its mouth. Small patches of minute teeth covering both the roof and tongue aid the fish in grasping and filtering the plankton and other material flowing into its mouth. However, much of the larger plankton particles and other material slip past the minute teeth and enter the throat. To protect the sensitive, inner openings of each gill from injury caused by large particles, an Atlantic herring has many long, slender structures stretched across its throat. The structures, called gill rakers, form a double row of stiff, bristle-like tissues that act much like a sieve by straining the water before it enters the gill openings. The gill rakers guard the extremely delicate filaments in an Atlantic herring's gills. The particles that successfully pass through the gill rakers enter the fish's gullet and are swallowed.

Young Atlantic herring grow rapidly. By May they are three inches long, and by September they reach lengths up to five inches. The young fish are attacked from virtually all sides. Fishes, sea mammals, and gulls feed on the closely packed schools. Again man appears in boats—this time to hunt the immature fish.

The Atlantic herring that escape their many predators relentlessly school around the waters they call home until their second year of life when they move farther offshore toward the open sea. Here they stay, growing and maturing, until they instinctively form spawning schools. Once again the powerful forces of nature drive the schools shoreward to spawn.

Again man, the predator, sets out in Norwegian fishing boat for young Atlantic herring

3. Atlantic Herring in History

One of the earliest known references to Atlantic herring was written by the Roman historian Solinus in A.D. 240 when he described the people of the Hebrides (islands off the northwest coast of Scotland) as "living on fish and milk." Historians have concluded that the fish mentioned by Solinus were undoubtedly herring. Later records show that by A.D. 836 Dutch merchants were purchasing salted Atlantic herring from Scottish fishermen.

Historians have also noted that three Germanic tribes, the Jutes, Angles, and Saxons, who jointly invaded and settled in Great Britain in A.D. 450, ate great amounts of Atlantic herring. In fact, the name herring comes from the German word *heer*, meaning army. So huge were the schools of Atlantic herring, and so precise were their swimming formations, that the early Germanic people called them an army.

Norwegians catching great numbers of Atlantic herring in the Baltic Sea had by A.D. 960 made the fish a staple in their diet. Legends state that numerous villages sprang up and prospered wherever a school of Atlantic herring made an appearance

Old print shows villagers drying fish in Norway

The herring plays an important part in the lives of the young people of today, as it did in those of their ancestors

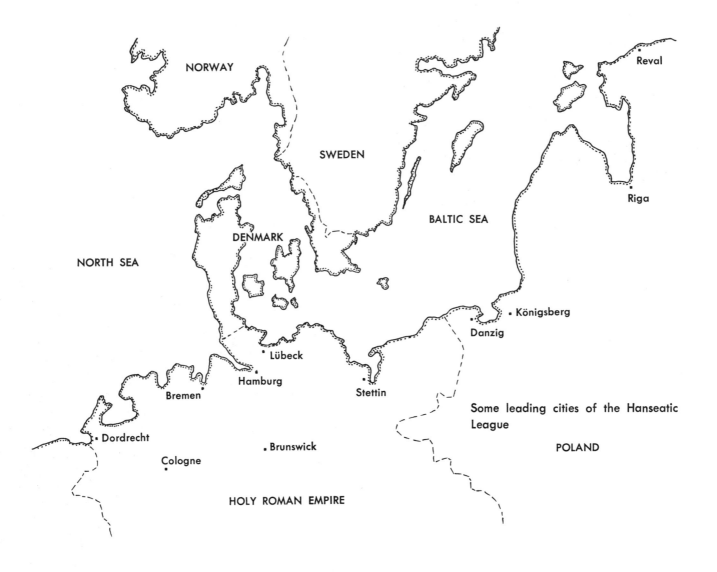

NORWAY

SWEDEN

Reval

BALTIC SEA

Riga

DENMARK

NORTH SEA

Königsberg

Danzig

Lübeck

Hamburg

Bremen

Stettin

Some leading cities of the Hanseatic League

POLAND

Dordrecht

Brunswick

Cologne

HOLY ROMAN EMPIRE

near the shorelines of Scandinavia, the British Isles, and what was later to become parts of Germany and the Netherlands. Amsterdam, the capital of the Netherlands, is believed to have been built on the bones of dead Atlantic herring.

In medieval times most Christians in Europe belonged to the Roman Catholic church. The many days of fast and abstinence were strictly observed. Eating of butcher's meat was prohibited two days every week, and during the forty days of Lent. Church fairs held during the Lenten observance sold great numbers of Atlantic herring to visitors and merchants. In the churches themselves prayers for successful catches were offered as early as the sixth century. Atlantic herring provided both an important industry and a vital food in the lives of the people of northern Europe.

In 1241, merchants of Hamburg (located on the North Sea), joined forces with merchants of Lübeck (situated on the Baltic Sea), to form an association known as the Hanseatic League. The purpose of the League was to protect the interests of the two cities in the Baltic Sea. A major interest of the cities was the catching of Atlantic herring and the selling of them throughout Europe. As Hamburg and Lübeck grew in wealth, other German cities joined the League. The formation of the Hanseatic League created, for the first time, a unified economic region in northern and north-western Europe.

For three centuries the League prospered, due in part to the sale and export of Atlantic herring. Salted fish were shipped to such distant cities as Rome in Italy. Lübeck became one of the most important commercial cities in Europe, and had for its town seal three Atlantic herring emblazoned on a gold shield.

But disaster struck the Hanseatic League in the early fifteenth century when the fish seemingly disappeared overnight. To this day no one knows exactly why the fish left the Baltic Sea, not to return till years later. With the loss of Atlantic herring the League's power declined.

Because Atlantic herring played such an important role in the religious observances, diet, and economy of the European people, new fishing grounds were sought by merchants and fishermen. The English and the Dutch, who for years had fished for Atlantic herring, became the leading contenders in the search for new fishing grounds.

England, surrounded by the sea, had early in its history turned to the sea for food. For centuries Atlantic herring had been a staple in the diet of the English people. The practice of having fishermen pay a tribute of Atlantic herring to a mayor of a port city, allowing them the right to fish in the waters near that port, was common in England.

During the Hundred Years' War between England and France, the English sent 500 cartloads of Atlantic herring, via a convoy of ships, to their troops attacking the French garrison at Orléans in 1429. The French attempted to capture the shipment and were routed. The battle became known as the Battle of the Herrings.

The Dutch, who had practically wrested their land from the sea, had, like the English, turned to the sea for food and wealth. Both the Dutch and the English had fished for Atlantic herring along their own coastlines in the North Sea for years. With the discovery of a new way of processing Atlantic herring, that staple in the Dutch diet became more valuable than ever. A Dutchman named Beuckels thought of the idea of gutting or cleaning out the insides of the fish and then packing the fish in

Old map of British Isles shows the North Sea, site of great herring conflict

barrels filled with a special sea-salt solution. This idea revolutionized the Atlantic herring fishery. Not only was the taste of the fish greatly improved but a buyer could be certain that all the fish in a barrel were processed in exactly the same way.

In 1540, Dutch fishermen first discovered huge schools of Atlantic herring just off England's coastline in the North Sea. By 1560 the Dutch had over seventy ships, averaging 140 tons, catching great numbers of these fish. So huge were the catches and so important were the fish to the Dutch that herring festivals were held at the beginning of each fishing season. When the ships returned from the sea brimming with the herring, flags were flown from official government buildings and people's homes, signifying the country's joy over the huge catches. By the end of the sixteenth century, the Netherlands was one of the most powerful and richest nations in Europe, due in part to the Atlantic herring.

England was upset and angered both with the Netherlands' increased trade and with the Dutch control of the Atlantic herring fishery in the North Sea. As one unknown Englishman of that day stated, ". . . to the great ignomy and shame of our English nation they (the Dutch) do vent our herring among us here in England, and make us pay for the fish taken upon our coast." At first England attempted to force the Dutch to pay tribute for the Atlantic herring caught off their shores. But the Dutch refused because they knew that England did not have the ships to back up the demand. In 1630, Charles I proclaimed England's sovereignty or complete control of the seas. To enforce the claim, England started a ship-building program. The first ship built, named the *Sovereign*, weighed 1740 tons and had 96 guns. Within a few years the English had a fleet of ships to enforce King Charles' proclamation.

In 1636 Charles I sent the newly established fleet to attack a band of Dutch fishing ships in the North Sea. The Dutch fishermen, standing little chance against the armed English ships, fled to their home ports. Tempers smoldered in both nations, and sixteen years later, in 1652, the fermenting emotions flared into a violent sea war that was to last two years. Samuel Pepys, the famed English diarist who was then

King Charles I of England ordered this medal struck after the Dutch agreed to pay for the right to fish for herring off England's North Sea coast

Secretary of the Admiralty, is credited by some historians with keeping the English navy intact and at sea during the conflict.

After many sea battles and skirmishes, England finally won the war and control of the Atlantic herring fishing in the North Sea. Within a few years England was catching and processing more Atlantic herring than all the European nations combined.

When the early settlers landed on the northeastern coasts of North America they soon discovered that Atlantic herring lived on that side of the Atlantic ocean as well as on Europe's side. Soon Atlantic herring became part of the diet of colonists from New England to Virginia. Small numbers of Atlantic herring were smoked by local fishermen and shipped to cities such as Boston, New York, and Philadelphia. Although Atlantic herring did not become as important a food fish in the New World as it was in Europe, a small fishery started to develop in Maine and Massachusetts.

The first major Atlantic herring port in the United States was Lubec, a small village situated on the Maine coast. In 1831, Lubec had some twenty smokehouses curing between 2000 and 3000 barrels of Atlantic herring each year. Other Maine villages such as Millridge and Steuben soon joined Lubec in preparing Atlantic herring for market. Between 1845 and 1865, nearly half a million boxes of smoked herring were annually shipped from Maine to many sections of the United States. But what made Atlantic herring a vital force in the economy of the United States was the opening of a canning factory in Eastport, Maine, in 1875. The fishery concentrated on catching small, immature Atlantic herring that could be packed whole, in cans, and sold as sardines. The word sardine originally meant a small member of the herring family called a pilchard. Pilchards, in ancient times, were especially prolific around the island of Sardinia in the Mediterranean Sea and so were commonly called sardines. Today, any of a variety of small fishes in the herring family are sold as sardines.

In the first half of the twentieth century wars and economic depression reduced the numbers of men and boats fishing for Atlantic herring. In both World War I (1914–1918) and World War II (1939–1945), the North Atlantic ocean, a major sea route between North America and Europe, became a "battlefield." Nations involved in the two great conflicts pressed men and fishing vessels into military service. Some boats served to evacuate soldiers and civilians from enemy-occupied land. Fishermen who

Modern sardine cannery in Maine. The first was opened in 1875

did not serve in the military but continued to fish were constantly open to attack by enemy ships and planes.

The period between the two wars saw the world plunged into the grip of a great economic depression. Money and jobs were scarce, and few new fishing vessels were built to replace the old, outmoded ones. The end of the second World War saw a rapid increase in world population and employment. Jobs were easier to obtain, but the increasing population reduced the amount of land necessary to feed the multiplying number of people. Mankind had no alternative but to turn to the sea for food.

Maine fishermen prepare boats before setting out for the fishing grounds

Fishing boats in a Maine harbor. Note seine net in stern at right

Nations such as Norway, Denmark, the Netherlands, the U.S.S.R., the Peoples Republic of China, West Germany, Sweden, Scotland, England, and later the United States and Canada began to build fishing fleets as the search for and catch of fishes, including Atlantic herring, increased dramatically.

4. Fishermen and Fishing

The thrill and excitement of the hunt, the huge catches, and the profit made from fishing for Atlantic herring have brought men to the sea for generations. No other fishes living in the same waters as Atlantic herring have been found in such large schools and caught in such great numbers. Skilled fishermen knowing the ways of Atlantic herring count on a good catch once they spot a school of the flashing, silvery fish.

The early Atlantic herring fishermen had a number of superstitions regarding a good catch of fish. An old Scottish proverb, "The only miserable herring fisherman is him with a full boat, for he cannae fill it," best sums up the fisherman's feelings. In England when a fishing trip was unsuccessful, effigies of men and women the fishermen felt might have caused the meager catch were hung in trees and burned. Many fishermen believed that the more fleas they had in their clothing, the more fish they would catch. Only a flea or two on their persons meant a poor catch. When Scottish fishermen left home to join their mates on board a fishing boat, they made sure that

36

A typical Irish herring boat working off the west coast of Ireland

Left: Boat full of herring docking at a Swedish port
Right: "A Haul of Herring," a chalk drawing by Homer

they did not pass anyone dressed in black because black signified few, if any, fish. A cardinal rule among fishermen was that no one was ever to mention the word salmon or rabbit aboard a herring ship. The mention of either word ruled out the possibility of a good catch.

Besides relying on superstitions, the early fishermen used their five senses to fill their boats with herring. The schools were located by the presence of circling, diving sea birds such as gulls and gannets. Men perched on the highest mast of a ship took turns scanning the sea for such telltale signs. Old-timers stated that when the sea "sort of browned over" there was bound to be a school of Atlantic herring there. Quite possibly the "browned over" appearance of the water was the result of Atlantic herring feeding on fields of plankton. Dead, churned up pieces of plankton that escaped the jaws of the fish floated to the surface, where the rays of the sun dried it. Other fishermen noted a "spot of oil" on the surface of the sea, which to them meant a passing school of Atlantic herring. Many fishermen were able to sniff out the schools by the odor of cucumber that permeates the air whenever herring are close by.

Another technique employed during the early years was the use of a weighted length of piano wire. After the wire was dropped overboard into the sea, a skilled fisherman who "had the feel in his fingers" could tell the size and direction of a school by the vibrations as the sensitive wire reacted to the fish.

The early European and American Atlantic herring fishery involved only a few ships. Small, sturdy, seaworthy boats called dories were lowered from the bigger or mother ship into the sea. The dories, manned by one or two men, used stop seines, nets with weights or sinkers attached to the bottom. The sinkers held the net on or near the bottom of the sea. Lining the top of the net were corks that kept the upper part of the net afloat.

Two fishermen, each having an end of the net in his dory, dropped the net over the mouth of a cove or inlet. Atlantic herring and other fishes in the cove were blocked or stopped from entering the open sea—hence the name "stop seine." When the seine

Right: Fisherman working in a dory pulls in an end of a stop seine

Far right: The large power block at the end of the boom is used today to haul a stop seine aboard a fishing vessel

became heavy with Atlantic herring the fishermen laboriously hand-pulled it from the sea, dropping the silvery-sided fish into the dories, now side by side. The heavily laden dories were rowed to the mother ship where the fish were loaded into nets dropped over the side of the ship and hand-pulled on board.

Stop seines are still in use today particularly in shallow inshore waters. The method of getting Atlantic herring on board the fishing vessel, though, has greatly improved. Machines have eliminated much of the brutal, back-breaking work done by the early fishermen.

Other early nets still in use are ring nets and drift nets. Ring-net fishing today involves two large vessels that work closely together. The ring net, approximately 320 feet long and 40 feet deep, is "shot" or thrown into the sea from the ships. Forming a ring or circle, the net is worked slowly into a smaller and smaller circumference by the two vessels. When the two ships are close together and the circumference of the net is relatively small, fishermen haul in the lower edge of the ring net. The trapped Atlantic herring are scooped from the net by a brail (a mechanically operated dip net) and then placed in the holds of the two ships.

To use drift nets, sometimes called gill nets, only one boat is necessary. Made of

Right: Ring nets drying at a dock in Nova Scotia. Note the floats that line the upper edge of the net

Below: Nova Scotia fishermen pulling in a ring net packed with herring

Norwegian fishermen scooping up herring from a drift net with a dip net

strong fiber, the net can be as large as sixty feet long and forty-five feet deep. Like stop seines and ring nets, drift nets have the upper edges rimmed with floats and the lower edges weighted with sinkers. Shot from a fishing vessel, drift nets are attached to the vessel or a buoy and hang like a drifting, netted wall in the sea.

Fishermen may shoot as many as eighty drift nets from one ship. Complete barriers of netting hanging vertically in the water may extend for more than three miles and make it difficult for Atlantic herring and other fishes to escape. The fishes' gills become entangled in the netting, and the more the fish struggle, the more entangled they become. At dawn fishermen pull the drift net with its catch aboard the fishing vessel.

In North America, before the Europeans settled the shorelines of the northeast, Indians made traps of thickets and brush to catch Atlantic herring. The traps, called brush weirs, were made by pushing poles down into the bottom of the sea. The poles were placed in an irregular manner to form a maze-like structure. Brush and thickets were interwoven between the poles, forming the trap.

Brush weirs were placed at the mouth of a cove or inlet, and as Atlantic herring swam into the cove they met the outer edge of the weir. Following the line of poles, the confused fish ended up in the inner pocket and swam in circles until Indians waded out at low tide to harvest them.

When fishing at night, the Indians "torched" for Atlantic herring with a flare made of birch bark secured to the bow of a dugout canoe. Several Indians steadily paddled the canoe while a fisherman, armed with a large dip net, straddled the bow. Atlantic herring and other fishes attracted by the light rose to the surface of the water. The

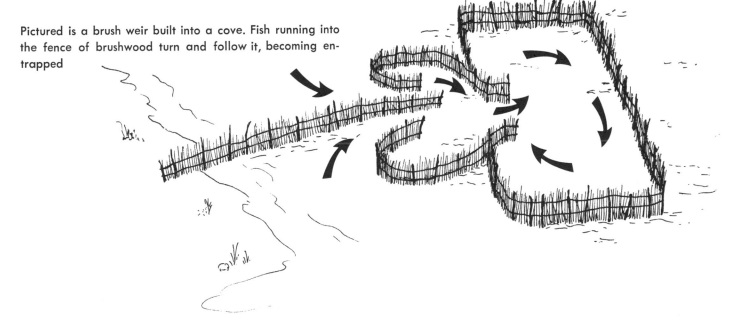

Pictured is a brush weir built into a cove. Fish running into the fence of brushwood turn and follow it, becoming entrapped

Left: Mid-water trawler unloading a "mixed" net of fishes onto the deck

Indian handling the dip net scooped up the fishes. Weirs and torching are still used as a means of catching Atlantic herring in Maine. Today, netting is stretched between the poles to form the weir, and oil-fired torches are used.

Mid-water trawling and purse seines are two methods commonly being used for catching Atlantic herring. A mid-water trawler's net is shaped much like a long, deep basket and is towed through the sea from the stern of a boat. Pulled through varying water depths for long periods of time, the net catches Atlantic herring and other fishes that are in its path.

Purse seines may be as long as 1800 feet and as deep as 450 feet. Shot from a vessel around a school of Atlantic herring, the vessel moves in a circular fashion around the school of fish. As the vessel circles, the bottom of the net is slowly pulled closed, mak-

Above left: Getting a purse seine ready

Above center: Purse seine is shot and the vessel starts to move in a circle

Above right: The bottom of the purse seine is closing

Right: Purse seine is closed

ing a purse. When the bottom of the net is completely closed, the trapped Atlantic herring are hydraulically pumped aboard either the boat or a carrier ship, so named because it can carry great amounts of fish in its hold.

As the methods of catching Atlantic herring improved, so did the ways of finding the fish improve. Electronic equipment such as sonar, radar, echo meters, and the like not only locate schools of Atlantic herring but also pinpoint the size and movement of a school.

Vessels using electronic devices have a tube projecting from the hull of the ship into the sea. Located on the topside of the vessel in a cabin or some other protected area is a recording device. The tube picks up information about the size and move-

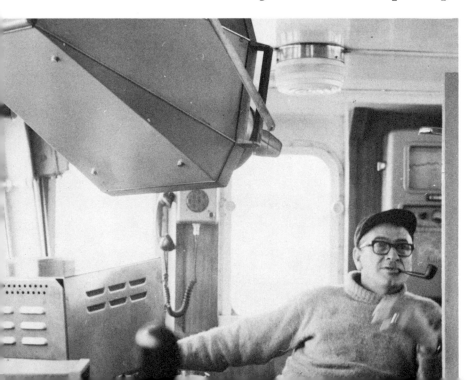

Captain of a fishing vessel surrounded by electronic equipment

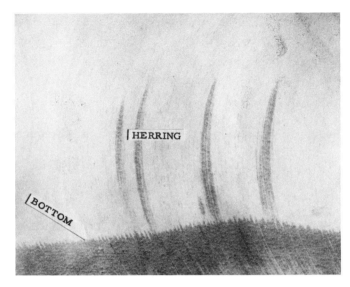

Graph showing herring schools along the northern edge of the Georges Bank. Depth of the bottom is 32 fathoms (192 feet). Herring extend from surface to about 15 fathoms (90 feet) over the bottom

ment of the school by sensing the vibrations of the fish. The information received by the tube is then transmitted to the recording device.

Some recording devices show a school of fish as a smudge on graph paper while others give the same information with bleeping sounds. A skilled technician reads the information and informs the captain when and where to shoot the fishing nets.

Fishermen in Maine have enlisted light airplanes to aid them in locating schools. The pilot of the plane scans the sea for diving gulls and other signs and relays the information via radio to the captain of the fishing vessel. The captain, following the directions of the pilot, heads his vessel toward the school.

Following the netting of fish, the captain puts in a call via shortwave radio to a cannery on shore to determine the price per pound of the trapped fish. After the price is mutually agreed upon, the captain of the fishing vessel tells the cannery his exact position on the sea. Immediately the cannery dispatches a carrier boat to the designated spot.

When the carrier boat arrives at the location, the captain of that ship inspects several samples of the netted fish. Once the fish are approved, a hose is lowered into the net and the fish are hydraulically pumped into a sluice (a trough for flowing water) on board the carrier ship. As the fish flow along the sluice, their fragile scales are easily rubbed off by the friction of the water against their bodies. Sieves in the sluice trap the silvery masses of scales. The lustrous scales, collected by crew members using bas-

Left: Carrier boats waiting at dockside to pick up herring.   *Right:* Hydraulically pumping herring aboard a carrier ship

Left: An insulated container being installed in a carrier ship. The container, filled with a mixture of ice and sea water, has extended the period that herring can be held without loss of quality from 12 hours to over 36 hours. The container can hold approximately 130,000 pounds of Atlantic herring.
Right: Herring being pumped directly from a net into insulated containers

kets woven by Passamaquoddy Indians, are later sold to manufacturers of imitation pearls, cosmetics, and fire-fighting foam.

The lifeless fish continue their journey along the sluice to the hold in the carrier boat where they are salted to preserve their freshness. A recent innovation in storing fish employed by some carrier boats is the use of large containers stored in the boat's hold which can be filled with ice and sea water to keep the fish fresh for a longer period of time. The fish are pumped directly into the containers.

Unloading herring with buckets rather than a hydraulic pump at a port in Nova Scotia

When all the netted fish have been pumped aboard the carrier boat the empty fishing vessel sets off to find another school of Atlantic herring. The carrier boat returns to port and the cannery.

Upon arrival at the cannery the fish are examined by state officials. If the fish are found unfit for human consumption they are used as bait for other fishes or turned into fertilizer or animal feed. If approved by the officials, the fish are pumped from the carrier ship through sluices or lifted by a brail to the cannery where they are soaked for several hours in tanks of brine. If a carrier boat uses containers, the containers are lifted by cranes from the boat's hold to the cannery where the fish are placed in the brine tanks. The brine keeps the flesh of the fish firm and heightens the taste. Following the soaking, the fish are placed on conveyor belts and brought to the packing room.

While some canneries precook sardines in hot steam, others fry or bake them, and some put raw sardines into cans and do the entire cooking process of the fish in the cans. No machine can do the job that the nimble and skilled hands of the workers do as they sort and place the fish in cans. If the sardines are cooked in the can, oil or sauces such as mustard or tomato are added before the can is sealed and the fish cooked. If the sardines are precooked, the oil or sauces are added after the precooking period and just before the cans are sealed. The canned sardines are automatically sealed by machines and placed in a pressure cooker where they are kept as long as an hour to sterilize the contents and complete the cooking process. The finished products, canned sardines, are now ready to be shipped throughout the United States and to many parts of the world.

Some sardines are cooked right in the cans

5. The Uses of Atlantic Herring

The flesh of fishes is divided into two broad groups—lean and fatty. Lean fishes include flounders and cod. Atlantic herring and mackerel are two whose flesh is fatty or oily. The fatty fishes spoil rapidly when removed from the water, and since their flesh does not freeze well they are prepared for future use by drying, salting, pickling, smoking, canning, or a combination of these curing methods. Atlantic herring are particularly delicious when cured because the oils in their bodies hold the flesh together and keep it moist.

Curing Atlantic herring by the sun is the oldest method of preservation for future use. The fish, split and gutted, are placed on wooden racks outdoors. The sun "draws" or dehydrates the body fluids. Once the fluids are drawn off completely, a fish may be kept for an indefinite period. To prepare it for the table, the fish must be soaked in water for a few days. Then it is boiled in fresh water until the flesh flakes.

Salting is done by packing the fish in dry, coarse salt. The salt, like the sun, draws or dehydrates fluids in the body and prevents spoilage. Also, the salt adds taste to the

View of a fishing village in northern Norway. Note the fish-drying racks to the left of the inlet

flesh. When no more fluids are being drawn from the fish's body, the flesh is cured. Salted Atlantic herring must be soaked in water for three days, with the water being changed four or five times a day. The fish is boiled briefly in fresh water and then is ready to be eaten.

Brining or pickling involves putting the fish in a strong brine solution for a certain period of time. This solution is made by mixing coarse salt with water until the liquid is briny enough to float an egg. The brine dehydrates the fluids in the body and adds taste to the flesh.

Smoking entails the use of salt and smoke. First the fish is soaked in a brine solution. When removed from the brine, the fish is hung on a rack in a smokehouse. Smoke from hardwood trees such as hickory or oak cures the flesh of the fish with a pleasing aroma and taste. Smoking takes time and patience because the process is dependent upon the weather. Humidity, winds, hot and cold days—all affect the smoking process. That is why today many cans of smoked Atlantic herring are chemically or artificially smoked. Atlantic herring are in no way comparable in taste to "true" smoked fish, and some people question the use of the chemicals that add the flavor.

Scandinavian people commonly smoke sardines before the fish are canned. An English, Irish, and Scottish favorite is the kippered herring. The fish, split down the back from head to tail, is placed in brine for a time—up to sixty minutes. Removed from the brine, it is lightly dried and then placed in a smokehouse for several hours. Another British favorite is the bloater. Bloaters are lightly salted but not split or gutted. The fish are briefly smoke-cured and must be eaten soon after curing because the flesh is perishable.

Left: Sorting and picking herring for shipment
Right: Transporting Atlantic herring to market in Lapland

Selling herring on a street in the Netherlands

A number of people, among them the English, Scotch, Irish, and Dutch, enjoy Atlantic herring fresh. The Dutch, Irish, and Scotch also prize herring swollen with roe (eggs) or milt (sperm). The Dutch call such herring *matjes*, while the Scotch and Irish call them matties. An English staple is gutted Atlantic herring grilled and served with or without mustard. A Scottish favorite is a herring dipped in oatmeal and cooked in hot fat.

The Dutch particularly like Atlantic herring caught in the early spring, which they call *nieuw haring*. The new herring are filleted (the flesh cut from the bones of the fish) and served with raw, chopped onions or gherkins. They are sold on street corners in Amsterdam and other Dutch cities, much as chestnuts and pretzels are sold in New York City.

The Germans prize *rollmops*. The herring is soaked overnight in brine and then the backbone is removed. The flesh of the fish is wrapped around a pickle and placed in a vinegar solution with sliced onions to be sold individually or packed in jars.

In the United States and Canada, although most of the Atlantic herring catch is packed into cans and sold as sardines, some of the fish are kippered or pickled. Kippered herring, either plain or in a variety of sauces, are packed in cans. Pickled Atlantic herring in cream sauce or wine sauce can be bought individually or in jars. However, it is the sardine that is a staple in the American diet. Some 125,000,000 sardines are eaten every month in the United States.

Beside being used as food for humans, Atlantic herring are processed into fish oil and meal and used as pet food and fertilizer. In some areas Atlantic herring are spread directly on farmland as a fertilizer. Sport as well as commercial fishermen use Atlantic herring as bait. Many lobster pots in New England and Canada are baited with fresh or salted herring. And nothing takes a cod better than a hook with a plump, fresh Atlantic herring.

Perhaps the greatest benefit that *Clupea harengus* provides is that it is one of the first links in the food chain in the sea. As we have seen, other fishes, such as bluefish, tuna, striped bass, pollack, and cod, feed heavily on Atlantic herring and they in turn are eaten by scores of humans throughout the world.

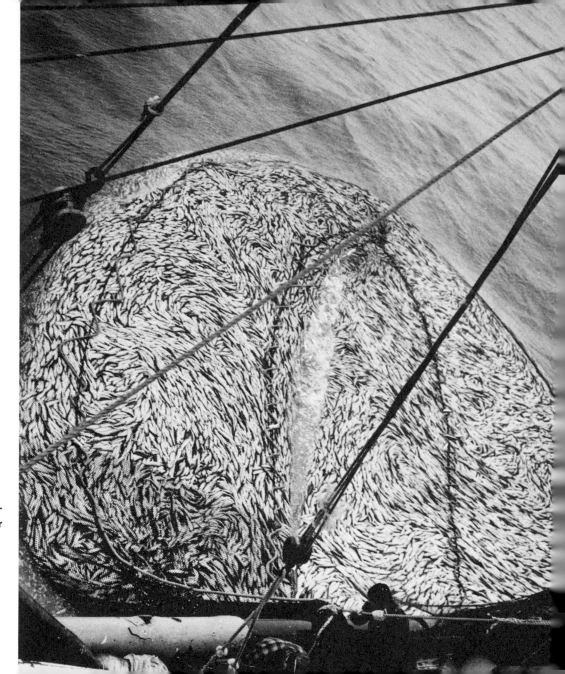

More than 100 tons of Atlantic herring taken by a mid-water trawler

6. The Decline and Future of Atlantic Herring

Tragically the numbers of Atlantic herring are dwindling. The instinctual schooling behavior of the species, which originally insured its survival, is today the basis for the decline. With improvements in the techniques and methods of hunting and catching following World War II, more and more Atlantic herring were, until recently, being brought back to port. Each ship brimming with mature fish reduced the number of males and females that spawned to produce a new generation of Atlantic herring. Further, the catching of large numbers of immature fish prevented them from maturing and having the opportunity to spawn.

In the early 1970's, the annual catch of Atlantic herring in the North Sea was less than half the amount of fish caught in the 1950's, and the stock of living fish is continuing to dwindle. So few are the Atlantic herring in the North Sea that fishermen recently left the area for the more fruitful waters off the northwest coast of Scotland.

In 1950 more than 185 million pounds of mature and immature Atlantic herring, caught in the inshore waters off New England—extending from the coastline to twelve miles out into the open sea—were brought into Maine ports. By 1960 the number of Atlantic herring taken in these waters had fallen to 152 million pounds. In 1965, 70 million pounds of fish were unloaded onto Maine docks, and by 1972 the number had fallen to under 45 million pounds. In twenty-two years, Maine fishermen and canneries had suffered a grand total loss of over 140 million pounds of Atlantic herring. With the decline in the catch of fish, the number of canneries in Maine fell from 51 in 1950 to 17 in 1974.

With the inshore number of Atlantic herring dwindling, Maine and other New England fishermen started to search offshore waters—twelve or more miles from the shore—for Atlantic herring and other fishes such as flounder and haddock. But many American boats, in the late 1960's and early 1970's, were not properly outfitted for this type of fishing. Offshore fishing demands large ships equipped with intricate electronic devices as well as refined methods of processing fish. Foreign fishing fleets, including Russian and West German vessels, are perfectly constructed for offshore

Present-day herring fleet getting ready to leave a Norwegian harbor

fishing. Many of these ships have lengths up to 300 feet with weights up to 3600 tons. These vessels are not only capable of catching huge amounts of fishes but they are also able to process the catch on board. A number of these ships, when they return to port, are ready to ship the processed fish to market.

Before March, 1977, great fleets of foreign ships caught vast amounts of fishes, including Atlantic herring, twelve miles beyond the shore of New England. At that time, United States fishing laws controlled the waters extending out twelve miles from the nation's shorelines. In March, 1977, The United States Fishery Conservation and Management Act extended the United States' fishing control of the sea to 200 miles from the shore. Since the enactment of the United States law many nations throughout the world have extended their fishing control of the sea to 200 miles.

Today, with one-half of the coastal nations having complete control of all fishing done within 200 miles of their shorelines, it is hoped by many fishery experts that the countries will work together to set up sensible fish-catch quotas for themselves and for other nations allowed to fish in their waters. If realistic catch quotas are alloted to all, there is a good chance that some declining species will make a comeback and flourish again. Also, species of fish that are now in good supply will remain so, if each nation is allowed to catch a reasonable number of each species and no more. However, if catch quotas are unrealistic or not observed, then it is quite possible that offshore fishing will decline just as rapidly as the inshore fishing has in recent years.

A number of scientists and fishermen believe that a complete study of Atlantic herring should be undertaken. Among the many things that these groups think should be analyzed are the spawning locations of the various races of Atlantic herring, the esti-

mated number of herring, and the factors governing the survival of the species. Many fishing experts believe that some Atlantic herring spawning in Canada's 200-mile fishing zone spend part of their lives in the United States' 200-mile fishing zone. The experts also believe that some Atlantic herring spawning in American waters spend part of their lives in Canadian waters. If this is true, then if either nation overfishes its own fishing zone it will reduce the number of Atlantic herring in the other country's waters, too. This problem is unique not only to Canada and the United States but also to other fishing nations, such as Norway, Denmark, and Sweden, that border one another.

Adding to the plight of Atlantic herring and all sea life is pollution. Industrial centers that discharge waste and chemicals directly into the sea or into rivers that flow into the sea pollute and kill many forms of marine life far from the industrial centers. Sewage-sludge dump sites and industrial-waste dump sites, set out into the ocean off the mainland, turn the sea into dead bodies of water unable to support marine life. Oil-tanker leaks and oil spills, killing or poisoning huge fields of plankton, upset the eating habits of all creatures that feed in the sea.

The time has come for the fishing nations to realize that if Atlantic herring are to survive man must learn to integrate his knowledge of technology with the forces of nature. No longer can unlimited numbers of Atlantic herring be taken and no longer can the habitat of Atlantic herring and other forms of marine life be polluted. Then perhaps ". . . to fish for the herring fish that live in the beautiful sea," as Eugene Field wrote in his poem "Wynken, Blynken and Nod," will continue to be a reality for untold generations of mankind.

INDEX